REWILD

Meredith Stricker

TP

PRIOR WORKS BY MEREDITH STRICKER

Anemochore, Newfound Press, 2018

Our Animal, Omnidawn, 2017

mistake, Caketrain Press, 2012

Tenderness Shore, LSU Press, 2003

Alphabet Theater, Wesleyan University Press, 2003

RECENT AND SELECTED TITLES FROM TUPELO PRESS

City Scattered by Tyler Mills

Today in the Taxi by Sean Singer

American Massif by Nicholas Regiacorte

April at the Ruins by Lawrence Raab

The Many Deaths of Inocencio Rodriguez by Iliana Rocha

The Lantern Room by Chloe Honum

Love Letter to Who Owns the Heavens by Corey Van Landingham

Glass Bikini by Kristin Bock

settler by Maggie Queeney

Bed by Elizabeth Metzger

Inventory of Doubts by Landon Godfrey

Tension : Rupture by Cutter Streeby, paintings by Michael Haight

Afterfeast by Lisa Hiton

Lost, Hurt, or in Transit Beautiful by Rohan Chhetri

Glyph: Graphic Poetry=Trans. Sensory by Naoko Fujimoto

I Will Not Name It Except To Say by Lee Sharkey

The Pact by Jennifer Militello

Nemerov's Door: Essays by Robert Wrigley

Ashore by Laurel Nakanishi

Music for Exile by Nehassaiu de Gannes

The Earliest Witnesses by G.C. Waldrep

Master Suffering by CM Burroughs

And So Wax Was Made & Also Honey by Amy Beeder

Salat by Dujie Tahat

Blood Feather by Karla Kelsey

Exclusions by Noah Falck

REWILD

Meredith Stricker

ISBN 978-1-946482-72-3

Library of Congress Cataloging-in-Publication Data
Identifiers: LCCN 2022016235 | ISBN 9781946482723 (trade paperback)
Subjects: LCGFT: Poetry.
Classification: LCC PS3619.T747 R49 2022 | DDC 811/.6--dc23/eng/20220520
LC record available at https://lccn.loc.gov/2022016235

Cover art:
Joan Mitchell (1925-1992). "Untitled," 1977.
Pastel on paper, 22 3/4" x 15 1/4", Private collection
Used by permission of Joan Mitchell Foundation.

Cover and text designed by Kenji Liu.

First paperback edition September 2022

Tupelo Press
P.O. Box 1767
North Adams, Massachusetts 01247
(413) 664-9611 / Fax: (413) 664-9711
editor@tupelopress.org / www.tupelopress.org

Tupelo Press is an award-winning independent literary press that publishes fine fiction, non-fiction, and poetry in books that are a joy to hold as well as read. Tupelo Press is a registered 501(c)(3) non-profit organization, and we rely on public support to carry out our mission of publishing extraordinary work that may be outside the realm of the large commercial publishers. Financial donations are welcome and are tax deductible.

This project is supported in part by an award from the National Endowment for the Arts.

ACKNOWLEDGMENTS

I am grateful to the following publications, editors and organizations who published and encouraged this work (sometimes in earlier versions):

Five Fingers Review	"The thin line"
	"That Beauty"
	"Commerce and the color of kingfishers"
	"A large black beetle tunnels head first into trail dirt"
	"There is no place to go but closer to leaves"
	"Lilies float in a pool like stars"
Guest	"The Radium of the Word"
	"Undertow"
Cutthroat,	"Human words"
A Journal of the Arts	"Leaf blower, dirt eater"
	"Sway like fish in waterlight"
	"The way I did not shape"

The series "*Human Words*" was awarded the 2018 Joy Harjo Prize and nominated for a Pushcart Prize.

The epigram for "*The unmarketable*" first appeared in *mistake*, which received the Caketrain Chapbook award.

Sections of "The Work of the Invisible" were part of a poem selected as a finalist for the Poetry Society of America Lyric Poetry Award.

"To make our way to that bright world again
we came out and looked up at the stars"

"From the most sacred waters I returned remade
in the way that trees are new, made new again...
pure and ready to ascend to the stars"

"Already were all my will and my desires turned
as a wheel in equal balance by the Love that moves
the sun and other stars"

DANTE ALIGHIERI,
LAST LINES OF *INFERNO, PURGATORIO, PARADISO*

The question is not so much: "will I go to heaven"
but will heaven exist if I live the way I live?
will there be a sky and greenness, will rivers and trout remain
will street vendors, hawks, human justice and wolves exist
will stars still have us to shine for?

CONTENTS

1   STARING INTO THE ATOM

Chronology . 1   1

Shot list for Rilke   2

You broke my heart   3

Chronology . 2   5

The radium of the word   7

Undertow   9

The Bees   11

The work of the Invisible   12

Flame hive   13

2   ASHES

The thin line   19

That beauty   23

3   DARK MATTER

Shopping cart   31

Chronology . 3   35

Dark matter   36

Chronology . 4   40

The rewilding   41

4   UNBUY YOURSELF

Logos   50

I'm making an inventory of the world   52

The swimmers of air   53

Stay close to clouds   54

Human words   55

Commerce & the color of kingfishers   59

5   NOTES   65

1 | STARING INTO THE ATOM

"— anything but this featureless tribe
that has the money now staring into the atom
completely blind, without grace or pity,
as if they were so many starfish"

WILLIAM CARLOS WILLIAMS, *PATERSON*

Chronology . 1

1948: Hiroshima
1948: the first shopping mall is built in the U.S.

Reality Television as Dante's *Purgatorio*
whose contestants undergo torment, purges, hang by straps
endure humiliation with strangers as roommates, devour insects
in Micronesia or get carved and hacked by plastic surgeons

consumer harrowing in search of algorithmic salvation

SHOT LIST FOR RILKE

: don't let him stare into space on camera

: don't let him turn his back

: the dead have many secret hand signals, be on the look-out

: get him to mingle with other long-lost celebrities —
  Brigitte Nielsen, Gary Coleman, the guy who goes after
  Walleye and Muskies on *American Sportsman* — but for God's sake,
  keep him focused, get a trainer in, get him under
  a tanning machine

: figure out his niche-market, go for the jugular

: if there is no niche-market, put him on roller-blades
  in a snake pit

: get him to barbeque steaks blindfolded with
  a Putin look-alike

: put him in a new home with a new wife
  and a pitbull in witness protection

: let this ache run over, let our yearning
  for celebrity expose us like light-sensitive emulsion

: toward the rarity of each unsocial-mediated self

YOU BROKE MY HEART

I was thinking of some of the messages Rilke will never receive:

— dentist called abt your appt tomorrow
— don't forget to pick up the olives
— your dry cleaning's ready

Little post-it notes of infinity, these outcast scraps of mortal
annoyances, fevers, artifacts, whispers and receipts were never
allowed near his poetry. When one is on "the path from inner
intensity to greatness", one doesn't collect coupons, worry about
toxic waste or pay attention to laundry. Rilke quarantined
himself from the sickness of money, the psychic germs
associated with the handling of money, the inglorious detritus
of veterinary bills, money squalls, anything remotely domestic.
This contamination he left largely to the phalanx of servants
employed by his aristocratic patrons, left the unsavory details
of money and credit cards for the rest of us to wallow in.
Rilke, you broke my heart on page 370
of *Life of a Poet*, when you called the writer Franz Werfel
          "Jew-boy" — a faceless taunt — stupid, ignorant,
product of your time?   a burr. stick. cudgel. abyss.

It's true, no one really knows how to live. I don't know
how to live. I don't know if redemption is possible, something
inside us like flowering, a kind of leakage, spillway over
rough concrete dam where a life washes outside its fixed
habits and resistance, its gaping absences, abscesses, horrible
mistakes, petty avoidances. I don't know if this life will be
enough to make me wise. I don't know if I can wake up.
I can only carry everyone with me, ferry every atom
like a fire brigade, like an ant. Rilke, am I carrying
you or are you carrying me? Readers are transitive,
are bound material, are more faithful than lovers.
You've been working on your after-life epic
through us, through stones, through bees, traffic,
through digital flickering, where you inhabit every
far-flung human aspect of buying, selling, trading
and also every non-human aspect. You're a free man.
Your poems are clouds, are economists, are ladders
— courting contamination, reveling in it as though
it were a field of thick, cadmium-yellow sunflowers.

Chronology . 2

circa 1901: Atoms are scattered in parallel tracks of infinity
by Einstein in his theory of relativity the same year Freud
publishes *Interpretation of Dreams*

Rilke leaves Russia distraught. Lou has written him off again
and now the flint-colored marshes at Worpswede become
consolation — two women in quiet rooms, in grassy starfields
listen so attentively, so fruitfully as he recites his poems
barefoot near candles and icons, fresh bread
a bowl of winter apples

No horsing around, he decides — to be a Poet is to be singular
A vessel on a wild sea, the "I" in your throat unsolid
as non-Euclidean matter
a gristle, a god

Destiny wrapt around your throat thick as a scarf of bees

1913: Gertrude Stein reinvents roses
1914-1918: WWI
1915: Kafka's *Metamorphosis* is published

c. 1914-1916: My grandfather takes photos at the Russian front
as an artillery officer and is wounded. The woods are sepia,
there is a chair made of branches, two men in uniforms with fur
collars bend over a make-shift table surrounded by pine saplings

We cannot hear the bombardment — perhaps there are still birds calling

1925: *The Bees of the Invisible*, Rilke sends a letter to his Polish translator
on the meaning of the Duino Elegies

1926: Rilke dies

1929: the cyclotron is born
Ernest Lawrence rigs up a $25 model of the cyclotron
to visualize an "atom-merry-go-round" where the energy of electrons
could be speeded up and deflected by circular mirrors in ceaseless motion
just as the merry-go-round of desire loops advertising
and planned obsolescence with bar codes as magnets
in the linear accelerator of appetite

"THE RADIUM OF THE WORD"

MINA LOY ON GERTUDE STEIN

Rilke's roses are nothing like Gertrude Stein's

Her roses resemble full-blown beef steaks dense with blood

Here's Stein with her shameless appetite, thunderous as rolling surf

Rilke hovers in the wings like a distant relative
someone who has come in temporarily from the rain
wearing the body uneasily

They share the gap between syllables

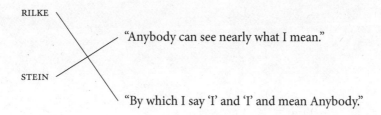

RILKE

"Anybody can see nearly what I mean."

STEIN

"By which I say 'I' and 'I' and mean Anybody."

and "I"? where "I" means "I"
as parachute swerve

presently the vista enlarges and we float
soundlessly over the water's surface
seeing ourselves reflected in the uncountable rifts
torn into its clarity

our bodies have become
not swans exactly

but their echo
                    the atoms of their echo

UNDERTOW

how the Invisible sanctuaries sight
protects
        the infinitely small
preserves us (fission-stained)
        from ourselves, from our burrowing into the visible
        like weevils in spilled flour who would unhusk
every atom, crack open every geode, leave nothing dark
and hidden and its own

        the sound of eagles over the Mississippi
                a biplane   treefrogs at dusk

              o star fall

give me
an alternate reading, the other story
                            back behind clouds

                hidden in ragged cloak, an island, an indigent
                            a wild animal, deep spring, a solace
your face swerves toward me
                like headlights across wheatfields
                            crows diving for grain

a Reader
an Undertow   a "you" without proof
                            without evidence
                                unseen across these words

THE BEES

"Our task is to stamp this provisional, perishing earth
into ourselves so deeply, so painfully and passionately,
that its being may rise again 'invisibly' in us.
WE ARE THE BEES OF THE INVISIBLE ...
The earth has no other refuge except to become invisible in us."

RILKE, IN A LETTER TO HIS POLISH TRANSLATOR, 1925

We are the bees, the bees, the zeroes, we are the oxygen
of the Invisible, the earth has blue, hydrogen, no other
refuge except this extinction web, no other refuge
except landfall, the grave beauty of the shore met
in holy increments of the real become Invisible in us
acres and acres of puffins sunning their wings
and city traffic taken wholly Invisible in us
with a tug of the rope sea lions vanish
whales phosphorescent beneath

    all day long the odors of the forest
              suffuse my skin, and now
      a lightning storm

        darker, arboreal the page erasing us as we read

THE WORK OF THE INVISIBLE

bees are like forensic workers who patiently sort
the patella from femur, ligament from tendon

those who archive and enumerate every star, cloud,
meteor, cave, fissure, island, inlet, leaf, genome,

those who comb through evidence past censors and silence,
somewhere, someone is counting, polishing, rectifying,

someone digs books out from rubble, drains
a bullet wound, measures for a new limb,

waxes a rusted screw-thread, reintroduces
wild salmon, sets a broken hawk wing

as bees hover and make contact with the fierce
edge of flowers, pull in and away like swimmers

like someone being born, the way a hummingbird careens
to the farthest reach of sky then plummets back in an arc

not caring if torn apart so ecstatic the magnet of this fall
that gives everything away in cascades of pollen

FLAME HIVE

the solid world porous as old plaster, a hive
    a comb, a cloudbank
        of atoms dragged out of their dark beds of matter
           where they had rested for eternity
    speeding the oscillation between matter and energy
            silence and jazz, a basket of fruit and the void
                Rilke dying pinned to his bones
        in a centrifuge of pain
           "I in flame. No one knows me."

        his gravestone of atoms stained
      with the pale lucidity of petals

sky of flame, earth of flame, the hunger of fire

      I try to imagine a world
            that cannot be blown up,
cannot be Abstracted, entirely irradiated
        by maniacs in power, by maniacs not in power

there is no other world,
so the imagination must create this one

2 | ASHES

"The difference between heaven and earth is infinite
yet the distance is minimal."

JOHN BERGER

THE THIN LINE

Every morning opening the newspaper, I am faced
with the thin line that divides disaster and deprivation
from a world of luminous wealth. Tuesday, January 29th,
for instance, bodies, many of them children, lie on the ground
They drowned in the canal trying to escape a weapons depot fire
and explosion in Lagos. Their heads are twisted in straw and dust
near the feet of on-lookers whose cries we cannot hear

And across two thin-as-breath lines: a cocktail shaker
about the same size as a body in the foreground
gleams quietly for $950 in stenciled silver
reflecting nothing in its lucent surface

I have learned to compartmentalize, to mentalize
I can tell the silver shaker is beautiful, in its way, but to see
it glisten there separately, something strange has to happen
to my sight

There are bodies on the ground, there is a pristine cocktail shaker
and two infinitely thin, poignant lines. The cocktail shaker
levitates to the foreground. It is untouched by the chaos, the loss
the weeping, the wet bodies, the smoldering munitions
Heaven would restore our sight. Earthly paradise
would dissolve the lines

Heaven is not a gated community. Silver is covered
with mud. Mud is covered with silver. The wounded
are cared for and made whole. The dead are washed
and mourned. We would leave nothing out
Not one atom of existence outcast

This is no dream

*"Parts of the canal were blanketed with hyacinths.
A woman's pink shoe, a baby's slipper and a bright orange
and red skirt floated among the plants."*

This is earth. This is paradise—how one grain of paradise
looks on a day in January. We are its eyes

THAT BEAUTY

"IT WAS GOLDEN, PURPLE, VIOLET, GRAY AND BLUE.
IT WAS THAT BEAUTY THE GREAT POETS DREAM ABOUT
BUT DESCRIBE MOST POORLY AND INADEQUATELY."

*General Farrell, War Department Release on the first atomic explosion
in New Mexico, 1945, a few weeks before the bombing of Hiroshima*

    desert flashes

    sidewinder flashes

    lightning, not even light

        but the cells of light

            newly washed photons

it was beautiful (they thought)

        unlacing light   and beauty

   will shatter stars, will pound us into dust

         the half-life of beauty is

     unbearable

       will never leave us

HIROSHIMA:

the temple has fallen from heaven

there was no sound no bells no trumpets no warning
the sky was clear

kindness like splinters of glass

"all day long people poured into Asano Park"

"the foliage seemed a center of coolness and life"

"because of an irresistible, atavistic urge to hide under the leaves"

the burns were not the burns of fire

everything collapsed as from the inside

a terrible wind

one doctor, a hospital full of people in torment

the experiment was a success

the pilot named the bomb
after his mother, in honor of his mother

this wasn't God, it was science

"an 'electric smell' given off by the bomb's fission"

"there were many dead in the garden"

"at a beautiful moon bridge, he passed a naked, living woman
who seemed to have been burned from head to toe"

they called it *genshi bakudon* — whose root character
can be translated as "original child bomb"

within weeks, the city was overgrown with greenness

it seemed as though the bomb had not destroyed
the plants, but somehow invigorated them

"everywhere were bluets and Spanish bayonets, goosefoot,
morning glories and day lilies, the hairy-fruited bean, purslane
and clotbur and sesame and panic grass and feverfew"

"it actually seemed as if a load of sickle-senna seed
had been dropped along with the bomb"

this is not about regeneration, it is about ashes

there is a bell ringing and it will not stop
and it makes no sound

it is wind, wind and ash

an eye within an eye within ash

dedicated to Taiken Yokoyama and to Kumi Uyeda
whose families were living in Hiroshima in August, 1945

quotations are from John Hersey's HIROSHIMA

3 | DARK MATTER

SHOPPING CART

at Safeway there were small gleaming carts for children
so we could learn how to roll the world before us while
our dreams sieved through the mesh like fine sand

"free gifts" in every box: a new kind of literacy
a new kind of freedom

in Hungary the paper is shiny and grain-colored
it smells of relatives and each scrap is precious as food
the entire surface covered with watery blue ink, there is hardly
any white space, unlike the limitless American frontiers

later we learn a shopping cart is more about its emptiness
than fullness

during the recent heat wave, water is brought onto the streets
of Barcelona for the pigeons and multitudes of wild parrots
their black tongues hanging out

it's not an art exactly, but acquired with patient, ceaseless
lessons in the appearance of choosing, cultivating an allegiance
to a brand of laundry soap, for instance, when all you want is
clean clothes

at the end of the war, my mother's uncle is shot dead as he steps
into the village street to greet the soldiers (the son overhearing news
of his father's death on a tram in Budapest)

a river in Jakarta connects to a semi-conductor facility in Sunnyvale

a street vendor in Lucca plays music on his cassette recorder

one day, I'm not sure when it happened, it becomes
perfectly normal to buy water, especially in California
then in other places

at the black market, my mother loses all their money
receiving in exchange newsprint wrapped in a few layers
of currency

the moon rises outside Barstow: ocotillo, cholla, santolina,
yerba buena

dictators' statues are corralled behind barbed wire outside
the city, a cacophony of fingers pointing into the air —
excess inventory of power in stone, bronze and ferro-cement

it becomes normal and entirely acceptable that a given
percentage of the population is permanently displaced
without a home, without credit

he crossed the border into Swizerland in the marshes
swimming under cover of a new moon

she found an amber ring in the forest where the family
took shelter after their train was bombed

people become refugees in their own country
with shopping carts replacing home

Chronology . 3

1867-1868: Cody boasts of killing 4280 buffalo. It took
the others only 30 years to finish off almost all the rest —
30 million? 60 million? More than half left to rot

"Late nineteenth century tanneries were thus an environmental
malignancy that destroyed bison, razed forests and fouled rivers"

The mass hunting of buffalos was not only an element of
advancing the Industrial Revolution and the Manifest Destiny
of railroads and profit, it also was a tool for ethnic cleansing —

Colonel Dodge: "Kill every buffalo you can ... every buffalo
dead is an Indian gone"

DARK MATTER

each buffalo could stand five to six feet at the shoulder,
could stampede at fifty miles an hour

the large dark eyes are the eyes of a Giotto saint

that hold a horizon of cropped-field hunger

split-fork timber, they hold bells and doves

bells and doves, wolves tossed into the air, howling

it's the thunder they make that rivets the attention

shakes souls, they are the loud Angels, the ones

clanging and bellowing with prophecy, they are

the rich ones, tallowed and tangled in wet, sweet smoke

fill your mind with sun-darkened prairie and you cannot

find the end of mind, of prairie

like a wide river (undying) or so it seemed to us

each one a candle flame, "grazing in undisturbed"

"possession" and in an instant, as a carbine clicked

the census like a wide-shadowed wingspan

ticked westward   the sun shook

     as they fell, the sun rose and

        set each day and each day forward

           the sun rose and set and it is as if their eyes are still

             wide open, are still   vast horizon

"Leather belts were the sinews of nineteenth century industrial production."
By 1890, the buffalo belting industry was valued at $8,600,000.

there's a man in a hat who poses like a small, temporary god

on a mountain of skulls at the Michigan Carbon Works

he's lifted one skull toward us — a large totem with the wide

curved horns of a lyre and it can't have been easy to climb

the skulls which shifted and crumbled and also stank, or purged

with lye, gave way to more skulls, it can't have been easy to render

the bones, to attain the richness of bones, the money of bones

to accumulate this necropolis of skulls for the hat market

in New Jersey, the tallow market, the tanning industry

heavy to lift, numerous as locusts — a massive act of translation

a trans-national act of transmutation turning the prairie, the beasts

the thunder, the tribes into the richness of ivory, of salt

of sap and the beautiful carbon of railroads

(*thousands of boxcars of bones*)

how lucky when the wind turned and the scent was lost

the wind that rushes now insensate through interstate

exchanges, dear fleet-foot, you gave us everything

and you were always coursing bright and red

     in our freeway blood   performing the mercy

        which inhabits grasses, stays alive in bones

           I keep hoping   (there is no hope)

           I keep trusting in bones

                  they do not lie   I keep hoping (there is no hope)

                 It is late and survival can drown us too

herd :
hoof — hardened — hoof cleansed   glistening
records — dismember   bunchgrass   orphic
ceaseless — earthworms   progress,   dirt,   progress
                    a fealty of little roots
        the sustenance of their bodies

how relentless commerce is
busy and global, large as the sky   but the world is not
yet emptied
                            scattered in bits like
sparrows
                            vowels

at the end of buying
it would take a forklift to carry   (my despair)
and there is absolutely
no charge for this

dark matter

the resources of dark matter

: its invisibility

: its overwhelming presence in the universe

: ~~what we don't see~~, as a path

: or resistance (imagine bird-flight)

Chronology . 4

1953-present: Since the creation of the Demilitarized Zone
at the end of the Korean War, a sanctuary has arisen spontaneously
from the killing zone of warfare that claimed the lives
of four million soldiers and civilians

Outside of human progress, the DMZ restored itself
in the space of less than a generation with the return of species
that were on the verge of extinction: musk deer, Asiatic brown
bears, Eurasian lynx, rare Goral sheep and rarer Amur and
Manchurian tigers, red-crowned cranes in wetlands
existent only because we are
absent

THE REWILDING

in the DMZ ravines north of the Kaesong wastes edging
south of the perfect ruler's pink and prisoned paradise

there is a climate paying no attention to us where cranes
repopulate serpentine deltas

another history than our own another spreadsheet than human
another profit another prophecy, chromosomal and intricate

nowhere is abstract unless we are abstracted
                        erasure held like a fierce lantern

RUINS IN FUTURE TENSE   THIS KEYBOARD, A PARTICULAR

BLUE LIGHT AT THE EDGE OF SHADOWS

when Orpheus
                lost in desolation and grief
        laments the double death of Eurydice, the bare land
around him restores itself as forest
one living,
unshielded tree at a time moves in closer to listen

mouth open, stained with tears

there is nothing not alive to us   even wasteland

no place free of desiring

            just as I want you / to read / me

                    and you only want / to build a nest in leaves

42

BRAINSTEM, SANCTUARY — HERE IS A LIVING ANGEL

— CORTEX, NEO-CORTEX

whose neurons bloom galaxies, star-maps while you're dreaming
and dreaming an andromeda-supernova-prefrontal incident eclipses
your sky-book's immense shimmering invasion

even if I forget, radiation remembers —
our isotopes won't desert us

(no hard-drive can hold this storm   (nor the stillness after

emptiness in earth takes the shape of their two bodies

MEMORY HEALS BY FORGETTING, OVER-WRITES US

then memory remembers again — a physical thing like a knot

what leaks is body
where train tracks converge the infinite

our eyes can't bear to see the visible, let alone the invisible

yet there is nothing that does not see us

JUST AS THE WORLD APPEARS TO QUIET DOWN

a tanker in the northern seas spills its cargo in violet glacial ice

her body arcs like a dolphin, rose-colored haunches curl and open

dripping stars milk firmament

the hairs on your arm, the raw blind mouth you tongue

try to open the gate without its consonants

conscience requires all the phonemes it can gather

sounds in another's voiceprint or chromatophoric gesture

flaking into awareness

INTO THE FIERY IMMENSITY OF LISTENING

a brain floats over debris like a surveillance satellite

unmanned missile, unexploded ordinance, now a bird calls

into places we cannot endure to touch or enter

everyday whited out   the news goes unconscious

and even though our minds cannot bear it
some part of us sees what is unseen

while in air crowded with the discourse of wi-fi
the not-yet extinguished

cranes open their wings into an unowned world

4 | UNBUY YOURSELF

I am burning with animals and greenness
        and a burning thing   cannot be placed
in a paper or plastic bag   cannot be downloaded
        or barcoded   cannot be held   only once, only
this time
        only wholeheartedly   in the risk
                                        of your eyes

LOGOS

Can we track the point in our post-millennial, unilateral
free-market culture when Logos became logos?

that is to say,

Logos — "Cosmic reason, affirmed in ancient Greek
philosophy as the source of world order and intelligibility"

or *Logos* — "the self-revealing thought and will of God"

now becoming most intimately for us a swarm
of marketing devices, corporate identities, brands

      common as pollen, rushing through
      our minds like sticky rainwater

           ↓

        Log-on

as an experiment: search on-line for

| things to buy | GO |

AltaVista search results in 2001: 6,187,977

Google search results in 2022: 8,770,000,000

that's an increase of approximately 8,763,812,023 things

an infinite market expansion on a finite earth
where shopping is possible at any instant —
in a meadow, shoreline or traffic

this wireless utopia inaccessible only to crows, whales
clouds, vagrants, the un-internetted, the unmarketable

•

item #3,146,000 of 8,770,000,000: vapor trail of a jet

if only, you, loved, me

I'M MAKING AN INVENTORY
OF THE WORLD

things you can buy and things you cannot:
        waves, dish-drainer, tree frog who moves
into the open when the rain comes

   how the proportions have changed — how rare, resistant
      the unbuyable has become

yellow flowered fennel covered in road dust
you can't pay for the dust, it comes for free
the roar of crickets on a back road —
what would you pay for this
night and its impenetrable
avalanche of stars

THE SWIMMERS OF AIR

two small birds flicker across the horizon
their wings stutter unevenly staggered
their flight shows us how to inflame our bodies
fling open our arms and spend everything we have
they are the swimmers Kierkegaard longed to meet
would travel any distance to meet
the swimmers of faith, the swimmers of air
faith in what? a god-in-leaves, marl pond
glycerine, carcinoma, leucocytes,
gazelles, the fleetness of gazelles,
oxygen we cannot see in the empty
space of air that loves us

                (flashpoint)

      eye—

            witness

as our language untethers from our senses (word) by fibered (Word™)

    imagine the arborescence of words,   their many tongues

  (pond-

        drifting)   their beautiful,

           unruly petals

STAY CLOSE TO CLOUDS

they elude the intentions of spokesmen
                              stay attentive to what happens

counting the dead, the displaced, the wounded
            the battered, on both sides, the maimed, the debt
                        the number of steelhead, echo blue
                  butterflies, drill press operators
and those who are hungry, those who just want to live
            non-union workers dressed in red, stalled
                        commuters, each of us requires
                  an accurate rendering, a reading
            whose force allows uncertainty
its exactitude

                        a weapon that undoes weapons

the complete truthfulness of fern fronds unfurling
                  like a shell, taking the shape that makes justice possible

HUMAN WORDS

"…the gate of heaven is everywhere" THOMAS MERTON

is heaven a chain link fence for a luxury car lot
              or the crook in a sleeping woman's arm
burned out light
nest in grass
a pause
in digging up the jack-hammered water main
              heaven as mended cloth
or armistice, cerulean blue canoe
                    a man lying dead drunk by a storefront
rusted winch, safe-house
a wren
        this small, saintly blot
                  this sad empty pen
what would you leave out,   what scrap-heaped
   holy, outmoded wreckage, what useless, unloved
      pile of bones
         and skin
            doesn't belong

leaf blower, dirt eater
        dust devil, brush whacker —
        why shouldn't I expect paradise in the roar
of a septic tank pump
as weeds glisten at midday with no trace of guilt, shame or agitation
        fields sheltered by dryness
                which shrives them bare

habitat restoration

        to heal human words

sway like fish in waterlight of aqueduct shallows
float green and unmetered in psalmed sound the hum
of electric wires strung across Wasco irrigation ditch
almond orchards outside San Ardo oil rigs fracked and churning over
delicate and hidden fault lines how strange to open like winged petals
drifting in air past crop-dusters
into Great Silence

the way I did not shape
the reticulate form of the thumbprint
that identifies me nor my DNA
nor last night's rain
that washed my dreaming
   I am moving without moving since the vastness
      of the sea moves for me
         is the actuality of the world
            as I watch a white sea bird take the devoted
               shape of disappearance
                  we are made of the same substance
                    our gestures coincide
                        where we lived, once, on earth

COMMERCE & THE COLOR
OF KINGFISHERS

how beautiful the caddis-fly larva transparency, blue jay wings

how beautiful the whipstitched air, our folded skin

•

now that the sky is a mall — wireless, satellite-saturated — no habitat
is immune to commerce, where swallows halo meadow grasses

we are hungry as field mice, in burr-stubble and brush, egg sacs glisten
the unsellable becomes an endangered species

(poetry for instance) where pelicans dive intent and dark

unincorporated ink, wily, unprofitable

down a dirt road, obstinate walnut trees slow in coming to leaf
do not concern themselves with efficiency

•

a white egret flies straight-legged, the undertow, magnificent, sexual
blue flowers call out to hummingbirds they've been waiting
all their lives for, blue flowers are the underside

of our desire and wait and wait for us to recognize them

to see ourselves in them and be unbought, unbound

large black beetle tunnels head first into trail dirt

shiny black beetle, can you dive into yourself?

you asked for consolation, here it is:
new grass, rain clouds, mitochondria, erosion's

silent effort, moon wearing thin

there is no place to go but closer to leaves

dive with the abandon of a crow
impossible to measure profit in flung wing
is this what happens when grammar runs out

                                        and we hear the sound the world makes?

                                lilies float in a pool like stars

                in this way breath tangles every living thing

        burning sensation, not unlike love

"*Everyday all over the world, the media network replaces reality with lies.*
Not, in the first place, political or ideological lies (they come later), but visual,
substantial lies about what human and natural life is actually made of.
All the lies converge into one colossal falsehood: the supposition that life
itself is a commodity ...

Imagine, suddenly, the substantial, material world (tomatoes, rain, birds,
stones, melons, fish, eels, termites, mothers, dogs, mildew, salt water) in revolt
against the endless stream of images which tell lies about them and in which
they are imprisoned! Imagine them, as a reaction claiming their freedom
from all grammatical, digital and pictorial manipulation,
imagine an uprising of the represented."

JOHN BERGER, *THE SHAPE OF A POCKET*

5 | NOTES

OPENING QUOTATIONS FROM DANTE:

"We came out ..." Dante, Canto XXX: translated by Robert Hass in
Dante's Inferno, edited by Daniel Halpern; "From the most sacred
waters ..." Dante, Canto XXX, *Purgatorio*, translated by W.S. Merwin;
"Already were all my will ..." Dante, Canto XXX, *Paradise*, translated by
Anthony Esolen

STARING INTO THE ATOM

"anything but this featureless tribe ..." William Carlos Williams, *Paterson*

THE BEES

"Our task is to stamp ..." Rilke, letter to his Polish translator in *Duino
Elegies*, translated by J.B. Leishman and Stephen Spender

YOU BROKE MY HEART

"Jew-boy" Rilke quoted in *Life of a Poet*, by Ralph Freedman

THE THIN LINE

"parts of the canal ..." *New York Times*, February, 2002

THAT BEAUTY

I am indebted to John Hersey's, *Hiroshima* as a powerful act of witness
from which the quotations in this series are taken.

CHRONOLOGY . 3

"Late-nineteenth century ...", "Kill every buffalo ..."
The Destruction of the Bison, Andrew Isenberg

DARK MATTER

"Leather belts ..." *The Destruction of the Bison*, Andrew Isenberg
other source: *The Journals of Lewis and Clark*

CHRONOLOGY . 4

sources: https://www.theguardian.com/environment/2008/jun/20/
conservation.wildlife

"*How wildlife is thriving in the Korean peninsula's demilitarised zone*", Lisa
Brady, The Guardian, 2012

THE REWILDING

This series owes much to the work of a long time friend, artist Yong
Soon Min and to the field of bio-semiotics, pioneered among others
by Thomas Sebeok, a semiotician and linguist, who also wrote a report
in the 1980's for the US Office of Nuclear Waste Management titled
Communication Measures To Bridge Ten Millenia, "discussing solutions
to the problem of nuclear semiotics, a system of signs aimed at warning
future civilizations from entering geographic areas contaminated by
nuclear waste": https://en.wikipedia.org/wiki/Thomas_Sebeok

"prisoned paradise" akin to Mar-a-Lago in its pinkness and
opulent disconnect

"chromatophoric": the ability of cells to change color, as with certain
animals who communicate via color change

THE UNMARKETABLE

"I am burning ..." from "click on this" in the chapbook *mistake* by
the author

LOGOS

definitions of Logos: *American Heritage Dictionary*

THE SWIMMERS OF AIR

"they are the swimmers ..." see Kierkegaard, *Fear and Loathing*